QUILT-O-GRAMS

8 CREATIVE KEEPSAKES TO STITCH & SEND

CHERYL MALKOWSKI

C&T PUBLISHING

Text copyright © 2008 by Cheryl Malkowski

Artwork copyright © 2008 by Cheryl Malkowski and C&T Publishing, Inc.

Publisher: Amy Marson

Creative Director: Gailen Runge

Acquisitions Editor: Jan Grigsby

Editors: Lisa Swenson Ruble, Kesel Wilson, and Cynthia Bix

Technical Editors: Nanette Zeller and Teresa Stroin

Copyeditor/Proofreader: Wordfirm Inc.

Cover Designer/Book Designer: Christina D. Jarumay

Production Coordinator: Tim Manibusan

Illustrator: Tim Manibusan

Photography by Luke Mulks, Diane Pedersen, and Christina Carty-Francis of C&T Publishing unless otherwise noted

Published by C&T Publishing, Inc., P.O. Box 1456, Lafayette, CA 94549

Adobe product screen shots (page 36) reprinted with permission from Adobe Systems Incorporated.

Microsoft Word and Windows Media Player screen captures (pages 25, 26, and 30) reprinted with permission from Microsoft Corporation.

Quilt images (pages 21 and 22) reprinted with permission from The Electric Quilt Company.

Library of Congress Cataloging-in-Publication Data

Malkowski, Cheryl

  Quilt-O-Grams : 8 creative keepsakes to stitch & send / Cheryl Malkowski.

    p. cm.

  Summary: "Create simple but special quilted cards incorporating the techniques of art quilts. Projects are divided into two categories: ones that take a day or less to create and those that take a weekend or less."—Provided by publisher.

  ISBN 978-1-57120-528-5 (paper trade : alk. paper)

  1. Patchwork--Patterns. 2. Greeting cards. I. Title.

  TT835.M271765 2008

  746.46'041--dc22

                                    2008006263

Printed in China

10 9 8 7 6 5 4 3 2 1

CONTENTS

INTRODUCTION: WHY QUILT-O-GRAMS?

Have you ever needed a gift that lets the receiver know he or she is someone special, but you just don't have time to make a whole quilt? Do you sometimes want to send a greeting card but know that two seconds after it's received it will hit the round file and never be thought of again? Or is there an art quilter inside you who wants to get out but is intimidated by the complex procedures required to make a true masterpiece? Quilt-O-Grams are perfect for all these situations.

Recently, I had the urge to communicate heartfelt thanks to a number of people for a job well done. Quilt-O-Grams were born that very day. They are small, envelope-sized fused quilts, backed with poster board for a written message. This was my opportunity to let my inner art quilter out! I could fuse down the elements of the project, quilt it to bring out the design, fuse the quilt to the poster board, add a fused binding and message, and pop these puppies in envelopes and into the mail! Voilà!

Small in size but not in sentiment or impact, Quilt-O-Grams allow you to experiment with the art quilt in a very nonthreatening environment. There is no worrying about how the back will look or whether it will lie flat, because it will be covered with stiff paper that will hide imperfections and flatten the project. With Quilt-O-Grams, you can unleash that inner artist, at least on a small scale!

Easy to make, easy to send, easy to hang, and easy to treasure, Quilt-O-Grams are the perfect little gift to give when you want to be remembered. The projects in this book are divided into two categories: simple Quilt-O-Grams made from one or a few pieces of fabric that can usually be completed in an afternoon or less, and more complex Quilt-O-Grams constructed from multiple fabrics that will take a weekend, more or less, to finish. Start out with an easier project or jump right into a more elaborate design—either way, I know you'll have as much fun as I did.

GET INSPIRED!

Everyday life is brimming with inspiration. It's all around us. But how can you use it in your quilts? I carry a tiny digital camera with me all the time so I can photograph flowers, people, and interesting architectural elements. Yes, that was me in the Louvre taking a picture of the floor by the *Venus de Milo*. The floor was just more interesting to me than her face, so what else was I to do?

Keep your mind open to inspiration as you go about your daily routine. You might be surprised by what will spark your interest on a given day if you let yourself really look at your surroundings. It could be the bowl of strawberries on the counter, the daylilies in glorious bloom, or maybe the chickadee sitting on an icy branch in November. You could pass an amazing bit of tile work on the side of a building or an interesting pattern in the stones on the street. You may see something on your computer screen that excites you. Don't resist these things. Take time to truly see what is in front of you, and you'll be surprised where that inspiration can lead you.

BE FEARLESS WITH COLOR

Nature is a lot braver with color than most of us are, and we should take our cues from that. Take the sunset, for example—have you ever tried to actually name the colors there? It's a great exercise. I was surprised to find a blue-gray right next to a bright golden apricot alongside an inky purple. That's not something I would have come up with if I were looking to my imagination alone for inspiration. But somehow, when we look out at the natural world, it all works, even when there are gray-greens next to chartreuse next to Christmas greens and browns, with dots of periwinkle, scarlet, and fuchsia.

Photo by Cheryl Malkowski

Inspiration can come from many diverse sources.

Photo by Mike Walters

The natural world can teach us a lot about daring color combinations.

SELECT FABRIC WITH AN OPEN MIND

Choosing the fabric to use in Quilt-O-Grams is pure adventure. Since the projects are small, you won't need much, but you may want to search each fabric for the perfect area from which to cut your selected piece. It could also come down to the realization that you have to go shopping for more fabric. Does that upset you? I didn't think so.

It helps to have several pieces of fabric to choose from for any given part of your project. You can audition each one to see if it is right for the spot where you want to place it. Be careful with fabrics that have a noticeable pattern in them, especially when working with faces. The fabric in the puppy's face in *Kodiak's New Toy* has a swirly dot pattern in it. Notice how the template was placed so that the dots were swirling up and away from his face on the right side and coming down his nose on the left side. If the center of the swirl had been on the other side of the nose, it would have been very distracting. Use the fabric's patterns to enhance your project.

Swirly dots enhance shape of Kodiak's face.

Be open to using fabrics in unexpected ways. Look again at *Kodiak's New Toy*. The dark blue background on the right side is actually part of a leaf, as are the top halves of the floor background. The trick here is to stop thinking of the fabrics as synonymous with the motifs on them, and start thinking of them only in terms of what colors they contain. In a Quilt-O-Gram, most of the pieces will be quite small, and the original motif will be practically unrecognizable.

Kodiak's New Toy, 9˝ × 6˝, by Cheryl Malkowski, 2007

GENERAL INSTRUCTIONS

Quilt-O-Grams are small, fused quilt projects designed to fit inside an envelope for easy mailing. They have stiff paper adhered to the back that is further held in place by the fused binding. The paper is used to make the project easy to hang and to give you a place to write your message. Thus, Quilt-O-Gram!

TOOLS

Quilt-O-Grams are made with regular quilting tools, plus just a few additions:

■ rotary cutter
■ ruler and mat
■ fabric and paper scissors
■ a small, sharp pair of scissors for cutting intricate designs
■ parchment paper or an appliqué pressing sheet
■ a stiletto
■ a chalk pencil
■ a water-soluble marker

If you have a sewing machine with some fancy stitches, this is a fun place to use them, but a straight-stitch machine will do for most projects.

FABRICS

Prints for whole backgrounds or motifs

When you are using a whole piece of background fabric for a Quilt-O-Gram, any fabric is suitable. For the individual design elements, there are more considerations because all the fabrics are fused down with a raw edge. Again, you can use whatever fabrics you like for the elements, but be aware that printed fabrics with low dye penetration may show a lot of white from the back of the fabric. These fabrics will probably need to be satin stitched or given some other creative treatment along the edges to keep those white threads from showing. Hand-dyed batik, and solid fabrics work very well because there is no other color trying to work its way out to the front of the project. My favorites are batiks because of their vibrant colors and tight weave, which makes for less fraying.

Hand dyes and batiks with tight weave

SUPPLIES

You will need some standard-weight fast2fuse, a stiff interfacing with fusible on both sides. The fast2fuse eliminates the need to add fusible web to the background fabric and the paper backing. It makes quilting and embellishing a breeze because it has so much body you don't have to be concerned with stabilizing your project, yet it is flexible enough to bend easily while you are stitching on it.

Fast2fuse is available from C&T Publishing and comes in convenient craft packs or by the yard.

Fancy threads and yarns are so fun to use on Quilt-O-Grams! You can use all sorts of shiny threads, like metallic, holographic, or rayon. They will add dimension and sparkle to your projects, so get ready to experiment with them. My favorites are the 40-weight high-sheen trilobal polyester threads by Superior Threads. They are heavier than piecing thread and shiny like rayon, but stronger. Use a 90/14 top-stitching needle for most of these decorative threads, or a 90/14 metallic needle for the more fragile threads.

Threads and needles

Other things you will need are poster board or 67-pound card stock cut to the size of your project and some fusible web for the fabric elements. Choose a lightweight fusible web that is meant to be stitched through and will not gum up your needle.

FABRIC PREPARATION

Follow the manufacturer's instructions for applying fusible web to the fabric you have selected for the shapes in your Quilt-O-Gram. Once the fabric has completely cooled, remove the release paper from the back by scoring it with the point of a pin across the middle of the paper. Bend the fabric at the scoring line and pull off the paper. This leaves you with fabric that has nice body for cutting out shapes. Save the release paper to use as an alternative to tracing paper, parchment paper, or an appliqué pressing sheet.

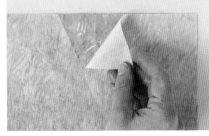

Score and pull off paper.

 tip

If you leave the release paper on the elements until after they are cut, it's much more difficult to remove it without fraying the freshly cut fabric, so just take it off to start with! You can store your leftover scraps of pre-fused fabric for use in future Quilt-O-Grams.

CHOOSING A PROJECT SIZE

One of the main objectives of making a Quilt-O-Gram is to have a project that is easy to put in the mail. While this sort of thing can be sent through the mail without any covering as long as it is hand stamped, I, for one, am unwilling to send these treasures unprotected. With that in mind, the best place to start a project is with the envelope size. There are many common envelopes readily available, even if you don't have a specialty paper store in your area. For example, a business envelope holds a 4″ × 9″ card easily. If you have a scrapbooking store nearby, it could be an excellent resource for reasonably priced envelopes in a variety of sizes.

Choose an envelope size and cut the fast2fuse about ¼″ smaller than the envelope. For example, for a 6″ × 9″ envelope, cut the fast2fuse to measure 5¾″ × 8¾″.

 tip

*A 6″ × 9″ padded mailer will measure larger than 6″ × 9″ on the outer edges. So, in a case like that, just start with the **stated** envelope size.*

tip

If you have chosen to embellish with buttons, crystals, or anything that gives the card sharp edges or points, include a sheet of bubble wrap (the kind with the tiny bubbles) in the envelope to protect both the project and the envelope.

ARRANGING AND ATTACHING THE FABRIC

Solid Backgrounds

1. Cut solid background fabric pieces ½″ larger on all sides than the fast2fuse.

tip

Unless you want to permanently enjoy your Quilt-O-Gram on your pressing surface, always remember to use parchment paper or an appliqué pressing sheet under the fast2fuse!

2. Place a piece of parchment paper or appliqué pressing sheet on the pressing surface, with the cut-to-size fast2fuse on top. Place the background fabric on the fast2fuse, and, following the manufacturer's directions, fuse the fabric in place.

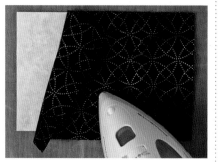

Fuse background fabric onto fast2fuse.

Pieced Backgrounds

1. Place a piece of parchment paper or appliqué pressing sheet on the pressing surface with the cut-to-size fast2fuse on top.

2. Arrange the background pieces on the fast2fuse in a pleasing arrangement, adjusting them so that they overlap each other at least ⅛″.

Arrange background pieces.

3. If you are using curved lines in your background design, overlap the pieces that will meet and cut them both at once. This will make a nice, clean, continuous curve that will easily fit together and overlap slightly.

Cut both curved pieces at once.

4. When all the pieces are arranged on the fast2fuse, place a piece of parchment paper over the top of your work to protect your iron. Fuse the background pieces in place.

Fuse layers with parchment paper on top.

tip

Don't worry if you miss an area. You can always cover it with another piece of pre-fused fabric.

5. Stitch around the raw edges of the background pieces to keep them from fraying later. They are easier to deal with now than when you have lots of shapes covering partial seams. A decorative stitch is fun here, if it fits with your design.

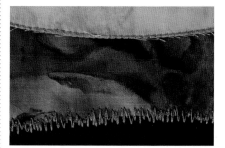

Secure background edges.

Shapes

There are several ways you can create shapes to form elements on your Quilt-O-Gram. Cut individual shapes from pre-fused fabric using templates or fabric motifs as your cutting guide. Small, sharp scissors are your best friend here.

Use small scissors to cut into tight spaces.

When cutting out multiples of the same shape (especially asymmetrical shapes), cut 2 or 3 at a time by accordion folding the fabric and cutting through all the layers at once. Folding the fabric creates more variety by reversing some of the images so your leaves or flowers do not look like they were made from cookie cutters.

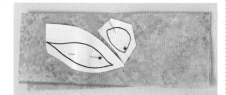

Use accordion folds to cut multiple shapes.

tip

It's OK to cut out more shapes than you think you're going to use. This is a good opportunity to audition different fabrics for different places. A shape you cut out now might be perfect in another project.

If several pieces form an element in your project, arrange them on top of parchment paper or an appliqué pressing sheet, fusible side down, before pressing. When you are satisfied with the arrangement, cover it with more parchment paper, and press lightly with a hot iron. After it cools completely, lift the design from the paper and place it on your project.

Lift cooled design.

Place all the elements on the background, and arrange them until you are happy with the layout. Cover them with parchment paper and press.

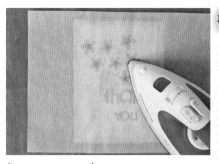

Arrange, cover, and press.

tip

Once you've pressed the shapes down, that's where they will stay. This is a good time to flip back your hair and say you meant to do that because that's the way you like it! If some pieces have shifted, you can camouflage the shift with quilting, thread painting, or other embellishments.

QUILTING AND THREAD PAINTING

Here comes the best part! Adding quilting and thread painting will make your Quilt-O-Gram come to life. You can quilt as little or as much as you like. A Quilt-O-Gram doesn't need quilting to hold it together, since it's fused, but this is an instance in which more really is more. The more thread you put on this project, the less important each stitch becomes, so if you're not an excellent machine quilter, not to worry—just add some more thread!

My choice is almost always to do free-motion quilting because it is faster and easier for me. But these projects are small and flexible enough that if you want to do straight-line stitching, you should have no problems. You could even use some of the specialty stitches on your machine to do the quilting if you desire. Below are some suggestions for easy patterns to machine quilt on a small scale. Because the designs are so small, they are easy to master by just moving the project with your fingertips. Use your sewing machine's quilting foot and set the machine to free-motion quilt.

tip

Try free-motion quilting with the feed dogs up and the stitch length set to 0, or as small as it goes. This gives you a tiny bit more control than with the feed dogs down. Most machines handle quite nicely like this.

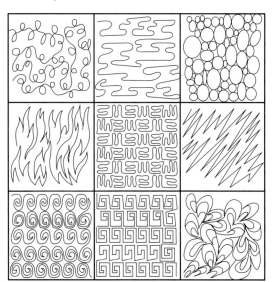

Simple quilting designs

Thread paint with a number of different thread colors to bring dimension to the shapes on your project. Let's look at how this leaf comes to life with simple straight and optional decorative stitching:

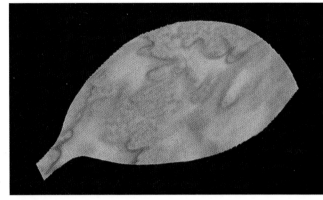

Shape fused onto background

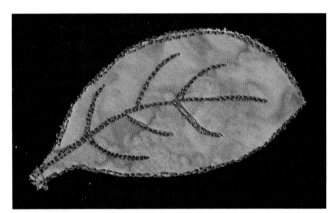

Dark green stitched around veins and edges

Lighter greens used for highlights and medium green for fancy outline

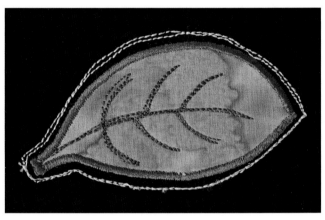

tip

I like to use a thin, bobbin-weight thread in the bobbin, such as Bottom Line by Superior Threads, and loosen the upper thread tension so the bobbin thread never shows on top. That way I am not winding eight different-colored bobbins for one 9″ × 6″ project!

When you finish thread painting, if the elements of the Quilt-O-Gram run together or don't stand out as much as you'd like, try adding two or three rows of black stitching around the shapes in the element. If that is not enough, stitch outside the black a few more times with white or a very pale thread. It's surprising how much difference that can make.

Black and white to set off shape from background; satin-stitch outline

EMBELLISHING

Quilt-O-Grams are perfect projects on which to experiment with crystals, buttons, beads, thick threads, and yarns. If you are not sure which kind of embellishment you will like, these small projects afford you the opportunity to investigate on a small scale before taking out a second mortgage to add on a new room for the beads and yarn. Your local quilt, sewing, and craft stores carry things like embroidered patches, iron-on beads, and fibers, often in little sampler packs.

A quick trip to your local scrapbooking store will really open your eyes to new ideas for Quilt-O-Grams! There are all sorts of embellishments that can easily cross over for use in this kind of project. And how about stamping words on with ink and rubber stamps? Use general-purpose ink, then cover the words with a pressing cloth, and press to set the color.

Stamped lettering from *Friends* by Cheryl Malkowski, 2007

Scrapbook embellishments

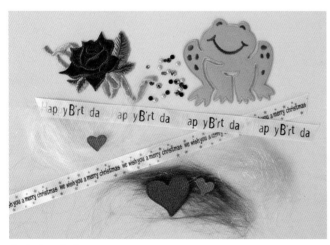

Craft shop finds

Crystals, Studs, and Buttons

There are crystals, studs, and pearls that either stick on or can be applied with a special tool or a household iron. They are so fun for flower centers or for making an accent trail like in the abstract quilt *Musical Inspiration* on page 29.

Crystal details from *Musical Inspiration*, page 29

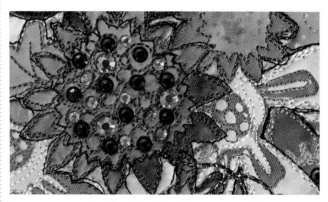

Crystal flower centers from *Thank You Bouquet*, page 43

Buttons can be used either as an accent or as an integral part of the design, as on the *'Tis the Season* Quilt-O-Gram on page 26. They can be sewn on or glued in place, but you may need to cut off the shank on the back of the button (if it has one) so it lies flat.

Close-up of snowman buttons from *'Tis the Season,* page 26

Couching Yarn

Yarns and heavy threads can be couched onto the top of your Quilt-O-Gram using the cording foot on your straight-stitch sewing machine or by just using a narrow zigzag stitch. Look for interesting nubby yarns, or try using more than one at a time.

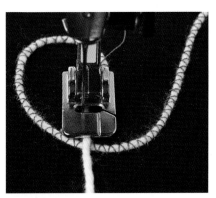

Couching yarn

tip

Remember, you can make as big of a mess as you want on the back of your Quilt-O-Gram, since it will be covered with paper in the end!

Bobbin Work

Bobbin work is a wonderful way to add dimension to your project or to cover the raw edges of print fabric. Quicker than satin stitching, it adds a unique, clean line around elements. It's sort of like couching from the back.

1. Begin by stitching on the top of the Quilt-O-Gram where you want the bobbin work to be, such as along the edges of a motif or as a trail across the project. Use a straight stitch with a thread color to match the project on top and a unique thread color in the bobbin so you can distinguish it on the back side of the project.

Colored bobbin thread is visible from back side of project.

2. Wind the heavy embellishment thread on the bobbin. Most machines can handle this kind of winding, but if your machine winds through the needle, wind your bobbin by hand. Load the bobbin with the heavy thread in the bobbin holder.

3. Load the top of your machine with thread that matches the color of the heavy thread in the bobbin. Turn the project so that you are looking at the *back side* with the unique thread color showing where to stitch.

tip

You may need to adjust the upper tension on your sewing machine when doing bobbin work. Before stitching your project, check your machine's tension by stitching on a small scrap of fast2fuse. If necessary, refer to your sewing machine owner's manual for instructions on adjusting the tension.

4. Pull up the bobbin thread on your first stitch so you can keep that heavy thread tail on the back of the project. To do this, lower the presser foot and take one stitch. Raise the needle and the presser foot, then grab and gently tug the top thread, pulling the bobbin thread up. The bobbin thread on the back of your work will be held in place and covered by paper later.

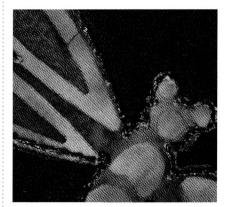

Pull up bobbin thread.

5. Stitch along the unique thread color lines and pull up the bobbin thread on the last stitch.

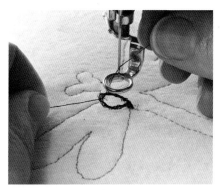

Bobbin work on project front

tip

I've used Razzle Dazzle threads by Superior Threads to add sparkle to my Quilt-O-Grams, but you could also use #8 perle cotton or embroidery floss for a subtler look.

ATTACHING THE BACKING

Once your Quilt-O-Gram is quilted and embellished to your liking, it's time to attach the paper backing. Use poster board for a single back, or if you want the card to open like a standard greeting card, use card stock. Consider preprinting the backing before attaching it to the Quilt-O-Gram (see Including a Message, page 15).

1. Cut poster board or card stock to the exact finished size you want. For a 6″ × 9″ envelope, that is approximately 5¾″ × 8¾″.

2. Place the Quilt-O-Gram wrong side up on your pressing surface with the poster board or card stock centered on top. Cover with parchment paper or pressing sheet and press with a hot, dry iron. It may take awhile for the heat to get through the paper, so be patient.

3. Trim the Quilt-O-Gram along the edge of the poster board, if necessary.

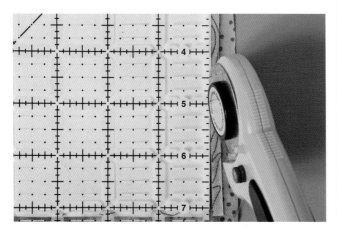

Trim along poster board.

❧ FOLDED CARDS

To make a folded card, cut card stock so that when it is folded, the doubled piece is the exact finished size you want. For a 5″ × 7″ envelope, if you want the fold on the long side of the card, cut the paper 9½″ × 6¾″. Fold it in half widthwise to measure 4¾″ × 6¾″.

ADDING A BINDING

1. Cut a rectangle of pre-fused fabric approximately 3″ × 12″. The rectangle should be at least 3″ longer than the longest side of your Quilt-O-Gram. Cut the rectangle into 3 or 4 binding strips ⅝″ wide.

2. Lightly mark, with a chalk pencil, the front of the Quilt-O-Gram with a line placed a scant ¼″ from the raw edges.

3. Use the marked line to align a raw edge of one of the binding strips to the front of the project along one side edge. Fuse in place, remembering to protect your work surface with parchment or a pressing sheet.

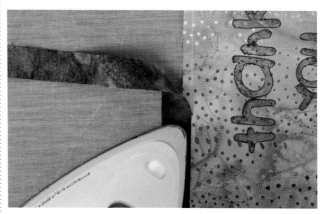

Press binding to front along marked line.

4. Along the same side edge, fuse the binding around to the back (paper) side by nudging it tightly over the edge with the tip of the iron, making sure to press it down smoothly. Stop fusing at the corner, being careful not to press the binding strip together.

 tip

A stiletto could really save your fingers here!

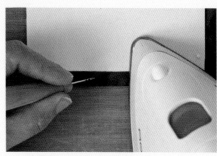

Press binding to back using stiletto.

5. For a mitered corner, cut the binding from the front and back almost to the corner. Be careful not to cut the binding strip all the way off.

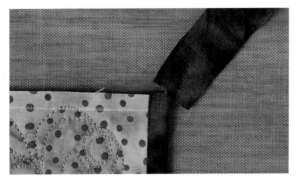

Cut almost to corner on front and back.

6. Wrap the binding around the corner along the next side, aligning the front with the ¼″ chalk line. Carefully cut a 45° angle to the end of the previous cut, and fuse in place. Fuse the binding to the back, where the miter is optional.

Cut out miter.

7. Repeat Steps 3–6 along each side edge to complete. When you reach the end of a binding strip, overlap a new piece, fuse it in place, and keep going.

✦ OTHER BINDING OPTIONS

For a simpler binding, skip the miters and just press down binding pieces that are the same length as the sides of the Quilt-O-Gram. Trim off excess fabric at the corners.

For a more quiltlike finish, try using ⅞″-wide prefused fabric and stitching it on as you would a normal quilt binding with a ¼″ seam allowance. Then press it from the front and back, clipping and mitering the corners as described in Steps 4–6 above, but only on the back side.

FINISHING WITHOUT A BINDING

Sometimes you may want your artwork to go all the way to the edges of your Quilt-O-Gram for a clean look. This technique can be used with either flat or folded cards.

✦ NOTE

In this no-binding approach, the edge is finished before the paper is attached.

1. Design and stitch your project, leaving the background pieces at least ½″ larger than the fast2fuse on all sides.

🪡 tip

Keep your iron clean by covering the fast2fuse with parchment paper, leaving room around the sides where you will be turning under the fabric edges. Or, when pressing the edges, be very careful not to allow your iron to touch the fast2fuse.

2. Turn the fabric edges onto the back side of the fast2fuse along 2 opposing sides. Fuse the fabric just along the edges of the fast2fuse.

Press fabric to back of fast2fuse.

3. On the back side, clip the just-fused fabric edge at the corner of the fast2fuse, as shown.

Clip fabric at edge of fast2fuse.

4. Clip excess fabric at each corner, and fuse the remaining 2 sides, as in Step 2.

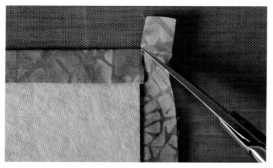

Trim excess fabric.

5. Cut the card-stock backing, single or folded, to match the finished Quilt-O-Gram (see Attaching the Backing, page 13).

6. Cut strips of ¼˝- to ½˝-wide fusible tape, or strips of fusible web, long enough to go around the edges of the paper backing. Fuse strips onto the paper along the outside edges.

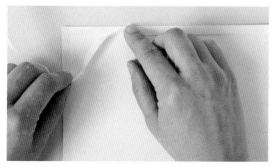

Apply fusible strips to paper backing.

7. Align and fuse the paper onto the back of the Quilt-O-Gram. The strips of fusible web will keep the backing attached where the paper touches the fabric.

INCLUDING A MESSAGE

Now it's time to add your personal message to the back of your Quilt-O-Gram. Since the back is paper, you won't need any special pens. How easy is that? Another option is to create a greeting on the computer and print it on card stock. Be sure to set your printer preferences for heavy paper.

OPTIONS FOR HANGING

There are lots of options available if you want to hang your Quilt-O-Gram. Ends of ribbon can be fused onto the back in small loops or one big bow. In the photo below, the large metal loops with the tab are from a hardware store. Glue the loops onto the back of the Quilt-O-Gram and cover the tab with a piece of pre-fused fabric. The small triangular loops are from a scrapbooking store. The black bars are self-adhesive magnetic strips.

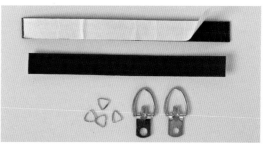

Possible hangers

Thread a piece of pre-fused ¼˝-wide ribbon or fabric through the loop, and cover with a piece of pre-fused fabric. Any thin, lightweight loop will work for this, such as the plastic loops that are available in drapery-making departments.

Thread the loop with pre-fused fabric.   Cover, securing the loop.

Self-adhesive magnetic strips or sheets are good for hanging Quilt-O-Grams on file cabinets or refrigerators. Just cut them to size and apply to the back.

tip

If your Quilt-O-Gram doesn't lie as flat as you'd like, press it one more time, and let it cool under a heavy book. It will comply!

ALL ABOUT THE FABRIC: PARROTS IN PARADISE

Parrots in Paradise, 6″ × 9″, by Cheryl Malkowski, 2007

A PIECE OF BEAUTIFUL FABRIC, A FEW SPARKLING CRYSTALS, A TINY DAB OF ANGELINA FIBERS, ALL QUILTED UP WITH SHINY THREADS—AND PRESTO! YOU HAVE YOURSELF A QUILT-O-GRAM.

Let's talk about how to choose a fabric for a Quilt-O-Gram like *Parrots in Paradise*. Look for a fabric with a beautiful motif that is about the size of your desired finished Quilt-O-Gram. Try to find one in which the desired motif is isolated enough that the next motif does not show on the front of your project. The fabric I used is perfect because the parrots are framed by the flowers, and the parrots don't repeat anywhere nearby.

You be the judge about what is acceptable to surround your motif. If necessary, you can cut out a paper frame the size of your project and move it over the surface of the fabric to find a place where the motif shows up the best. A solution for a crowded fabric is to fuse web to the back of the motif, cut it out, and use it on a simpler background.

Use cut-out frame to audition fabric.

Fabrics themselves can be very inspiring. Sometimes all you need to get a project going is a piece with an interesting motif. You can embellish it with yarns and threads or beads and crystals. This is a fast and simple way to make a card and let the fabric designer do most of the work, whether you're using a realistic motif or an abstract design.

Fabrics with interesting motifs

MATERIALS

- ▦ fast2fuse: 6″ × 9″
- ▦ Fussy-cut fabric: 7″ × 10″
- ▦ Pre-fused binding fabric: 3″ × 12″, cut into 3 strips ⅝″ × 12″
- ▦ Card stock: 6″ × 9″
- ▦ Decorative threads
- ▦ Pink and yellow Angelina fibers
- ▦ 3mm hot-fused crystals
- ▦ Setting tool or iron

ASSEMBLY

See General Instructions, pages 6–15, to fuse the fabric to the fast2fuse, to embellish the surface, and to attach the binding to your Quilt-O-Gram.

WORKING WITH ABSTRACT FABRIC

For this kind of abstract project, choose a fabric with an interesting pattern that you can stitch around, filling areas with different kinds of quilting and using different threads in different areas. Feel free to add some simple shapes, like the circles in *Bubbling Stream*, to add more texture and interest to the piece. I used Razzle Dazzle thread to do some bobbin work on the circles and some of the lines and added holographic thread just for fun. Allow yourself to play with the embellishing until you're pleased with the project, using just thread as I did, or adding ribbons, yarns, and crystals. Finish by adding paper backing and binding. For specific details, see General Instructions, pages 13–15.

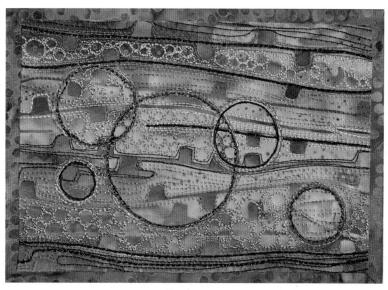
Bubbling Stream, 7″ × 5″, by Cheryl Malkowski, 2007

REFRIGERATOR ART FOR GRANDMA:
HOUSE

House, 9″ × 6½″, by Christina Knight, age 6, quilted by Cheryl Malkowski, 2007

HOW FUN WOULD IT BE FOR GRANDMA TO GET
YOUR CHILD'S ARTWORK IN THE MAIL, REFRIGERATOR
READY AND MORE DURABLE THAN A PAGE FROM A
COLORING BOOK?

Simple children's drawings can be made into very quick Quilt-O-Grams that will have special sentimental value for grandparents or other loved ones. Regular crayons work on fabric, as do fabric markers, and can be heat set and used for a single-fabric Quilt-O-Gram. With a magnetic strip or two attached to the back, it can be refrigerator ready in no time!

MATERIALS

- fast2fuse: 9″ × 6½″

- White muslin: 10″ × 7½″

- Pre-fused binding fabric: 3″ × 12″, cut into 3 strips ⅝″ × 12″

- Card stock: 9″ × 6½″

- Freezer paper: 12″ × 9″

- Crayons or fabric markers

- Variety of threads

- Self-adhesive magnetic strip: 18″

ASSEMBLY

1. Press the freezer paper, shiny side down, onto the muslin, and trim off the excess paper. This will give the child a firm surface on which to color.

tip

Using a pencil, draw a box on the fabric the size of the completed project minus ½″ in length and width, and ask the child to stay within the lines. This way the artwork won't get cut off with the binding.

2. Let the child draw until he or she is happy with the picture.

tip

If your child tends to use a light hand when coloring, you may want to go over the design with the same color crayon so it will show up better.

3. Remove the freezer paper from the back of the fabric.

4. Place the artwork right side up on your pressing surface. Cover it with a pressing cloth or a paper towel and press. This will remove the excess wax from the crayons or heat set the fabric markers.

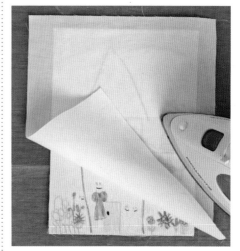

Press to set colors.

5. See General Instructions, pages 6–15, to fuse fabric to the fast2fuse, for tips on using thread to outline and enhance the drawing, and to attach a binding to your Quilt-O-Gram.

6. Cut the self-adhesive magnet into 2 pieces 9″ long and secure them on the top and bottom of the back of the Quilt-O-Gram.

7. Send it to Grandma and wait for her to brag about her little one!

THAT QUILT YOU NEVER WANTED TO MAKE: PINK & GREEN MINI

Pink and Green Mini, 7″ × 7″, by Cheryl Malkowski, 2007

HERE'S A QUILT I NEVER WANTED TO MAKE. NOT BECAUSE IT'S NOT BEAUTIFUL, BUT BECAUSE HAND APPLIQUÉ AND I ARE NOT CLOSE FRIENDS. IF I WERE MAKING THIS QUILT FULL-SIZE, I WOULD BE CONFLICTED BECAUSE I'D FEEL COMPELLED TO PUT MORE TIME INTO IT THAN I WOULD WANT TO GIVE. THIS WAY, IT WAS FINISHED IN AN AFTERNOON, AND I STILL GET TO ENJOY IT!

What if you could make a miniature of that complex New York Beauty quilt or the fancy Baltimore Album quilt without doing a bit of piecing or appliqué? Now you can! With the Electric Quilt (EQ) program, or similar quilt designing software, you can design a quilt any way you like and then print it out on fabric. (For more information on Electric Quilt, see Resources, page 47.) You can use that fabric as a single-fabric Quilt-O-Gram and quilt it with a very fine thread.

One more thought for you: How fun would it be to send a Quilt-O-Gram along with a full-sized quilt that you give as a gift? If you took a good, straight-on photo of your quilt, you could print it on fabric, make a Quilt-O-Gram, and add your greeting to the recipient. Or you could keep the Quilt-O-Gram for yourself to remind you of the quilt that got away!

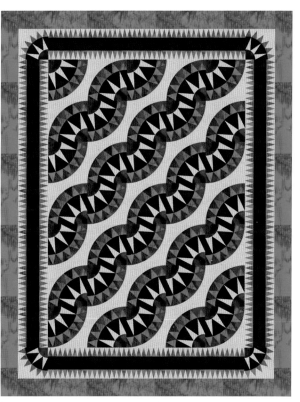

Quilt image from Electric Quilt 6 (EQ6)

Quilt image from Electric Quilt 6 (EQ6)

Quilt image from Electric Quilt 6 (EQ6)

MATERIALS

- fast2fuse: 7″ square
- Printable fabric for inkjet printers: 1 sheet, 8½″ × 11″
- Pre-fused binding fabric: 3″ × 10″, cut into 4 strips ⅝″ × 10″
- Poster board: 7″ square
- EQ program or other quilt design software
- Inkjet printer

DESIGNING, PRINTING, AND SAVING THE IMAGE

1. In EQ6, design and color a quilt to your liking. It can be ridiculously elaborate because you don't have to sew it.

> *tip*
>
> *For a Quilt-O-Gram with no binding, make the outer border extra wide to wrap around the fast2fuse.*

2. From the File menu, select Export Image. You will be prompted to name your file, so type in a name and save it as a JPEG file. Put it in a folder you can find later.

3. Once you hit the Save button, a new pop-up screen will appear. Choose the size you want your Quilt-O-Gram to be—in this case, 7″ × 7″.

4. Choose a resolution for printing. I recommend at least 300 dpi.

5. Choose whether or not to have the lines around the patches and blocks printed in black. If you don't want them, just click on the boxes and the checks will disappear.

6. Click OK. Your quilt image is waiting for you in the file where you placed it.

Exporting image (EQ6 screen shot)

7. Follow the fabric sheet manufacturer's suggestions for placing the printable fabric sheet in your printer, and print your image onto the fabric.

EQ printable fabric sheets for brilliant images

8. Once printed, it's important to set the ink colors to keep them from bleeding. Follow the fabric sheet manufacturer's suggestions or use a product such as Bubble Jet Rinse by C. Jenkins to make your work more permanent.

> *tip*
>
> *When looking for printable fabric sheets, be sure to get ones that are compatible with your printer type and fabric that is suitable for your Quilt-O-Gram. There should be many varieties and brands available at your local quilt shop or craft store.*

ASSEMBLY

1. Remove the backing from the printable fabric sheet.

2. Trim around the quilt image, leaving about ½″ all around. Carefully center the fabric onto the fast2fuse, and fuse, matching the quilt edges with the fast2fuse edges. (See Arranging and Attaching the Fabric, page 8.)

3. Quilt with a fine thread, and embellish as desired.

4. See General Instructions, pages 13–15, for directions on finishing your Quilt-O-Gram.

5. Brag about finishing this fancy "quilt" in a few hours.

CHILD'S NAME CARD: JACK

Jack's Name Card, 9″ × 4″, by Cheryl Malkowski, 2007

JACK'S ROOM IS ALL ABOUT FROGS, SO LET'S LOOK AT HOW TO GO ABOUT MAKING A NAME CARD FOR HIM IN THIS EXAMPLE.

Are there little ones in your life who would appreciate being able to personalize their space? Quilt-O-Grams make fun little name cards. These can be hung with ribbons that are glued or fused onto the back of the card.

Follow the directions on the facing page to create names using your word processing program, or draw the letters freehand if you like.

Brady's Name Card, 9″ × 4″, Cheryl Malkowski, 2007

Melia's Name Card, 9″ × 4″, Cheryl Malkowski, 2007

You can decorate the name card with fabric motifs that accent the nursery theme. Another idea is to quilt words that relate to the meaning of the child's name into the background. The name Zoe means life, and you'll see that word in the quilting of this spunky little preemie's Quilt-O-Gram name card.

Zoe's Name Card, 9″ × 4″, Cheryl Malkowski, 2007

Detail of *Zoe's Name Card*

MATERIALS

- ◼ fast2fuse: 9″ × 4″
- ◼ Fusible web: ¼ yard, 18″ wide
- ◼ Background fabric: 10″ × 5″
- ◼ Pre-fused letter fabric: 8″ × 4″
- ◼ Iron-on frog patch
- ◼ Pre-fused binding fabric: 3″ × 12″, cut into 3 strips ⅝″ × 12″
- ◼ Poster board: 9″ × 4″
- ◼ Pins or spray basting
- ◼ Computer

ASSEMBLY

1. See General Instructions, page 8, for directions on applying background fabric to your Quilt-O-Gram. Fuse a single-piece or simple collage background onto a 9″ × 4″ piece of fast2fuse. If you choose a collage, you may want to do some decorative stitching where the fabric edges meet. It's easier to do that now than to work around the letters later.

2. Choose a font for the name and decide whether you will use all uppercase letters or both uppercase and lowercase. In Microsoft Word (version 2007), start a blank document, click on the Insert menu, and then click on Picture > WordArt.

3. Double-click on the first option, a simple black-outlined font (or whatever font you prefer). Choose your font in the largest size and type your child's name. Click OK.

4. Right-click on the WordArt box when it opens up on your document, then choose Format WordArt. Under the Size tab, type in 2.5″ for the height and 7″ for the width, or choose the length that fits your plan. Jack's frog is really big, so I made his name 5″ long.

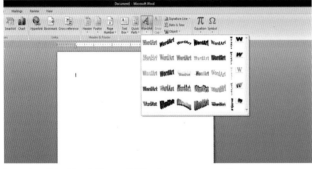

Inserting WordArt (Microsoft Word screen capture)

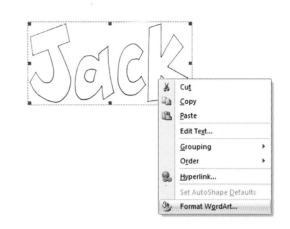

Right-click on image and Format WordArt (Microsoft Word screen capture).

Size to 7″ × 2½″(Microsoft Word screen capture).

5. Print the WordArt document onto copy paper.

6. Pin the paper letters to the right side of the pre-fused letter fabric, and cut around them.

 tip

For quick placement of the letters, use basting spray to temporarily adhere them to the fabric. In a well-ventilated area, place the paper letters right side down in a cardboard box, and spray the backs of the letters with basting spray. They're now ready for placement.

7. Arrange the letters on the fused background, cover with parchment paper, and fuse in place. Add whatever fabric motifs, stitching, and embellishments you like.

8. See General Instructions, pages 13–15, for directions on finishing your Quilt-O-Gram, and add a hanging device such as a grosgrain ribbon glued to the back.

HOLIDAY GREETINGS: 'TIS THE SEASON

'Tis the Season, 7″ × 5″, by Cheryl Malkowski, 2007

WHEN THE OCCASION COMMANDS MORE THAN A SUPERMARKET GREETING CARD, SEND A QUILT-O-GRAM! THE RECIPIENT WILL REMEMBER IT LONG AFTER THE PAPER CARDS HAVE BEEN TRASHED. WITH EMBELLISHMENTS LIKE THE BUTTONS USED IN THIS DESIGN, THE PROJECT IS ALMOST DONE ALREADY.

You can brighten someone's holiday with a Quilt-O-Gram greeting card. On page 28, you'll find an assortment of holiday shapes that you can copy or trace, then cut out for many occasions. You can also find your own shapes from clip art. You could even just use a beautiful holiday-print fabric, and stitch around it or embellish it with couched yarns or bobbin work.

Fun and beautiful holiday prints

 tip

You can find usable, non-copyright-protected shapes in clip art collections right in your word processing program. In Microsoft Word, go to Insert, then click on Picture > Clip Art, and search for "holiday."

Finding clip art (Microsoft Word screen capture)

If your greeting card calls for words on the front, you could cut them from pre-fused fabric, stitch them on with bobbin work, write them on with a fabric marker, stamp them on with ink, or quilt the words right in. If your machine has an embroidery function, you could use it to write your message in decorative thread. The fast2fuse alone is stiff enough that you won't need any stabilizer for embroidery.

Write your greeting with thread.

MATERIALS

- fast2fuse: 5″ × 7″

- Sky fabric: 8″ × 5″

- Ground fabric (light): 8″ × 4″

- Tree fabric pre-fused: 6″ square

- Pre-fused binding fabric: 3″ × 10″, cut into 3 strips ⅝″ × 10″

- Card stock: 10″ × 7″ for folded card

- Buttons: 6 snowflakes and 3 snowmen

- Sparkling thick thread, silver studs, and white Angelina fibers for the sky detail

- Glue

ASSEMBLY

1. Prepare the background by cutting a pleasing curve out of the sky and ground fabrics. See page 8 for details.

2. Fuse the background to the fast2fuse, trim, and stitch along the raw edge of the curve.

3. Pre-fuse the tree fabric before cutting out the shapes.

4. Use the Holiday templates on page 28 to cut one of each of the evergreen trees from pre-fused fabric.

5. Fuse the trees onto the background.

6. Stamp, write, or stitch your greeting, then quilt and add thread details.

7. See General Instructions, pages 13–15, for directions on finishing your Quilt-O-Gram.

8. Glue the buttons in place.

Check out the Gallery on pages 42–46 for more ideas on Quilt-O-Gram greetings. Look in coloring books, appliqué books, and clip art files for more designs than you have time to make.

Holiday templates

ABSTRACT ART:
MUSICAL INSPIRATION

Musical Inspiration, 9˝ × 6˝, Cheryl Malkowski, 2007

THIS PROJECT CAME FROM WATCHING THE SHAPES AND COLORS
DANCE ACROSS THE COMPUTER SCREEN WHILE I PLAYED A CD.
I CAPTURED AN IMAGE I LIKED TO USE FOR INSPIRATION.

For me, even abstract art usually has to come from some sort of inspiration. Often, it is just an idea of a color scheme or other element that impressed me in a quilt or other medium. It is helpful to expose yourself to many different art forms. For example, the flow of one color into the next in handblown glass is fascinating to me. And paintings from impressionist, expressionist, abstract, and modern artists show us some possibilities of what can be done. Of course, we don't want to reproduce their work, but we can draw on their collective inspiration to come up with our own.

Sometimes abstract inspiration can be as close as your computer. First, you can look at all sorts of artwork on the Internet by doing a search and looking through galleries. Second, the dancing, mesmerizing visualizations in media-playing programs such as Microsoft Windows Media Player and iTunes are fabulous places to find new ideas.

MATERIALS

- fast2fuse: 9″ × 6″
- Fabrics to match selected image (or printable fabric sheet; see Tip on page 22) for background
- Pre-fused fabrics for design elements
- Pre-fused binding fabric: 3″ × 12″, cut into 3 strips ⅝″ × 12″
- Poster board: 9″ × 6″
- Fusible web
- Computer
- Inkjet printer

CHOOSING AN IMAGE

1. To "catch" one of these images, open the music program and select View Visualizations. Put in a CD or play tunes from another source. If you have a fast Internet connection, you can listen to an online radio station.

2. While the music is playing, images will dance across the screen. Watch carefully, and when you see something that intrigues you, pause the music.

3. Use the Print Screen button or feature on your computer to capture the image. This sends it to the clipboard, ready to be pasted into any graphics program you have, such as Photoshop Elements or Paint (which comes as a Windows accessory). From there you can crop off the knobs and buttons that you don't need and adjust the image to the size you want.

ASSEMBLY

1. Decide what you like about the image and want to use. In the image below, I liked the patchwork-like background and the 2 swirls of sticks that were layered and changed colors from the inside to the outside. Those were the elements I focused on when assembling the resulting Quilt-O-Gram.

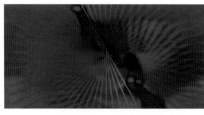
Microsoft Windows Media Player image

2. Your assembly process will vary based on the design you choose, but I used a commercial hand-dyed fabric that changed colors from one end to the other for the swirling sticks. I collaged a background that loosely resembled the image and then added lots of quilting with fancy threads and crystals just for fun.

3. See General Instructions, pages 6–15, for directions on finishing your Quilt-O-Gram.

 tip

Another way to use these programs is to capture the image and then print it straight onto a printable fabric sheet to use for your Quilt-O-Gram. The resulting fabric makes a fun background or fabric to stand alone and embellish as you desire.

Blue-green Microsoft Windows Media Player image

Blue and red Microsoft Windows Media Player image

tip

For more ideas on using photos in realistic or abstract designs that are adaptable for Quilt-O-Grams, check out More Photo Fun *by Cyndy Lyle Rymer and Lynn Koolish, and* Altered Photo Artistry *by Beth Wheeler and Lori Marquette, both available from C&T Publishing.*

FANTASY FLOWERS: DO ZINNIAS GROW LIKE THAT?

Do Zinnias Grow Like That?, 5¾″ × 8¾″, by Cheryl Malkowski, 2007

FOR FANTASY FLOWERS, BEGIN BY CHOOSING A SINGLE

FABRIC OR A SIMPLE COLLAGE FOR THE BACKGROUND.

THEN MAKE YOUR FLOWER AND LEAVES FROM THE SHAPES

PROVIDED OR MAKE SOME NEW SHAPES OF YOUR OWN.

ANYTHING GOES WHEN IT'S ALL MAKE-BELIEVE!

Whole worlds of fantasy come out of ordinary everyday shapes such as circles, which are my personal favorite, as well as ovals, teardrops, footballs, squares, and triangles. It doesn't take any great artistic genius to cut out these shapes in different sizes. Combining motifs from fabric and geometric shapes expands the possibilities even more!

Simple shapes

 tip

Be sure to include a wide range of sizes in the shapes you choose for your Quilt-O-Gram. A shape repeated in different sizes is much more interesting than a glob of same-size shapes. It's easier to get a pleasing design with a variety of sizes.

On the facing page you will find an assortment of shapes to trace that will get you started making fantasy flower Quilt-O-Grams. You'll find the beginnings of daisies, roses, tulips, and total fantasy flowers there. I have numbered the shapes but not labeled them, because some of them are multipurpose. In one case a shape could be a petal, and in the next, a leaf. Consider each end of a shape and decide what you want in your flower.

tip

You may find that you'd like to supplement your flowers with motifs from a favorite fabric. You can add leaves, animals, or bugs—whatever works for you.

Fussy-cut motifs

Fussy-cut leaves add contrast.

If you get all your shapes fused onto the background and you still don't feel you're getting the impact you want, not to worry. Read the quilting and thread painting tips on pages 9–12 to make the elements of your Quilt-O-Gram stand out. It is surprising how much difference the thread work can make in these projects.

MATERIALS

- fast2fuse: $5\frac{3}{4}$″ × $8\frac{3}{4}$″
- Background fabric: 7″ × 10″
- Flower and binding fabric: fat eighth
- Leaf fabric: 7″ × 7″
- Scraps of yellow and orange
- Fusible web: $\frac{1}{4}$ yard, 18″ wide
- Poster board: $5\frac{3}{4}$″ × $8\frac{3}{4}$″

CUTTING

Pre-fuse all the fabrics you'll be using except the background. Use the full-size templates on page 33 for the shapes.

Flower fabric:

Cut 5 of piece 1.

Cut 1 piece each of 2, 3, 4, 7, 14, 17, 30, 32, and 39.

For binding, cut 3 strips $\frac{5}{8}$″ × 12″ or $\frac{5}{8}$″ wide to total 34″ in length.

Leaf fabric:

Cut 1 piece 7″ × $\frac{1}{4}$″ for stems.

Cut 1 piece each of 25, 30, and 41.

Cut 2 pieces each of 34 and 35.

Yellow and orange scraps:

Cut 1 piece each of 6, 8, 10, 11, 14, 16, 17, 20, and 30.

Cut 2 pieces each of 9 and 12.

Fantasy flower shapes

Do Zinnias Grow Like That? **master template**

ASSEMBLY

1. See General Instructions, pages 6–15, to assemble and finish your Quilt-O-Gram.

2. Use the project photo, page 31, and the master template, at left, as placement guides for your fantasy zinnia.

3. Place the background fabric on the fast2fuse, and fuse.

4. Arrange the main design on parchment paper with the master template underneath as a placement guide. Overlap the shapes as indicated with the dashed lines. Fuse the design as one piece (see Shapes, pages 8–9).

5. Cool and lift the design from the parchment paper, and place it on the background. Place any remaining shapes on the background, cover the piece with parchment paper, and fuse everything in place.

6. Quilt and thread paint to accent the flower, outlining the shapes with black and very pale thread. Use the project photo for shading location ideas.

7. See General Instructions, pages 13–15, for directions on finishing your Quilt-O-Gram.

USING A PHOTO: HIBISCUS

Hibiscus, 9˝ × 6˝, by Cheryl Malkowski, 2007

THIS QUILT-O-GRAM WAS MADE FROM A PICTURE OF A BEAUTIFUL HIBISCUS TAKEN AT A RESORT IN CANCUN. THE SIDEWALKS WERE LINED WITH THEM, AND THIS REMINDER OF THAT TIME ALWAYS MAKES ME SMILE!

Sometimes you will want to actually reproduce a photo as accurately as you can, and sometimes the goal is to convey the mood or use the photo as a springboard for a project. Let's talk about the steps for making a photo into a realistic Quilt-O-Gram. Photo-enhancing software makes transforming favorite photographs into Quilt-O-Grams much simpler. It breaks down a complex photo into simple shapes that can be made into templates for your project. Without the help of a computer program, the easiest thing to do is to blow up the photo to the finished project size and get it printed. Then follow the steps in Preparing a Pattern, page 38, starting with Step 3.

> *tip*
>
> *Don't be afraid to crop away part of the subject in the photo. The closer you get to the subject, the more intimate and personal the final outcome will be, whether you're working with animal, vegetable, or mineral. You can give the impression that you're showing viewers something they wouldn't have otherwise seen.*

Blueberries

Blueberries cropped—wow!

USING A COMPUTER PROGRAM

Making templates from your photograph is greatly simplified if you have access to a computer program such as Photoshop Elements. (For more information on Adobe Photoshop, see Resources, page 47.) You can crop the photo to the exact size and area you want and apply a filter to flatten the spaces in the photo.

The computer is much more objective about where the colors change than is the eye, and I find it is much easier to decide how to make the templates for patterns after turning the photo into something more like a cartoon. I try a couple of different things before deciding which filter gives me the image I like best.

> *tip*
>
> *Different versions of Adobe Photoshop may require different steps to get the same results. Check your program's Help option for specific details.*

1. First save the photo under a different name so you can keep your original.

2. Go to Filter > Artistic > Poster Edges. This will bring up a screen with options about how many layers to make. There are options about how detailed you want to get. Try adjusting the *posterization* level downward and the *edge intensity* and *thickness* upward. This worked perfectly for the blueberries.

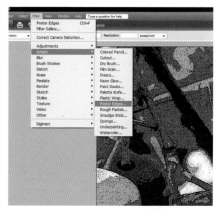

Filter > Artistic > Poster Edges (Adobe Photoshop Elements screen capture)

> *tip*
>
> *If you don't like what you get, cancel it. The image will return to its previous condition.*

3. Next, try Image > Adjustments> Posterize. I usually go with 4, but you'll have to decide what works for your project, so try different settings, resetting the photo between each attempt.

Image > Adjustments > Posterize (Adobe Photoshop Elements screen capture). I used the posterize filter to make the *Hibiscus* pattern on page 38.

Photo by Cheryl Malkowski

Photos are all different, so there isn't one surefire way to produce a traceable rendering of every photo, providing you with all you need to draw the outline and color boundaries. The varying amounts of color and value contrast within each photo call for different procedures to achieve the desired end. So if you still don't get anything you can easily trace, try the following:

4. Filter > Artistic > Cutout **or** Filter > Stylize > Find edges. You should be able to get something out of one of those that is easy to trace. Sometimes I use a combination of 2 filters, printing out 1 for the edges and 1 that shows the boundaries of the different colors within the edges. Just make sure you start with the photo already cropped to size.

Sometimes using Cutout filter is perfect (*Kodiak's New Toy*)!

Photo by Cheryl Malkowski

Water lily photo

Use Find Edges filter for when you just need outline (*Water Lily*).

5. When you find something you like, save it with a note in the name about what you did to get the photo to its current condition. For example: *hibiscusposterized 4cropped.jpg.* Then, when you have several alternatives to choose from, audition each one, and print out the one that is best for tracing.

6. Print it out on plain paper in draft mode so the colors will be lighter and the edges will be easier to see. Use this rendering instead of an actual photo in the following steps.

Water Lily, 9″ × 6″, **by Cheryl Malkowski, 2007**

PREPARING A PATTERN

Photo by Cheryl Malkowski

Hibiscus photo

Here are the steps to take to make this hibiscus photo into a Quilt-O-Gram using Photoshop Elements. Follow these steps when making your original photo Quilt-O-Gram.

1. In Photoshop Elements, crop the photo to 9˝ × 6˝ and use the Image > Adjustments > Posterize method of turning the image into a cartoon.

2. Print your altered photo in the desired size using the draft mode of printing.

3. Use a black fine-point marker to outline the different elements in as much detail as you desire, remembering that you will have to cut these shapes out. Keep this as your master pattern.

Outline sections on your master pattern.

4. Lay tracing paper over the outlined photo, and trace the master pattern with a pencil along the marker lines.

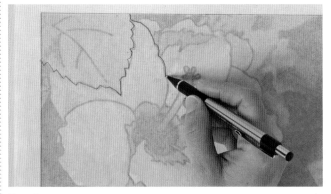

Trace image.

5. Number the pieces and make notations about what colors you'd like them to be. For example, if your background has more than one piece, number them B1, B2, B3, and so on. Also use these pattern pieces to note what layer the piece is on, and whether it has an area that will slip in behind another. Mark these edges with a dashed line to be used as a cutting aid. Place the dashes on the inside edge of the pattern piece that will have the underlap. When you cut the fabric pieces, the dashed line will indicate the edge that will need extra fabric for the underlap.

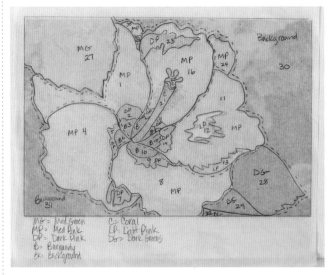

Number pieces and mark details.

6. If a large area will be cut from one piece of fabric but still has details in it that will be filled in with thread or fabric, mark those lines with water-soluble marker directly on the fabric. Wash the lines out by spraying the piece with water after you've embellished it with thread.

 tip

> *It is helpful to put a sheet of white paper under everything so you can more easily see the details you need to add to your piece. If that doesn't do the trick, try putting your piece up to the window or using a lightbox.*

MATERIALS

- fast2fuse: 9″ × 6″
- Fusible web: ⅝ yard, 18″ wide
- Medium green: 4″ square
- Dark green: 4″ square
- Medium pink: fat eighth
- Dark pink: 4″ square
- Light pink: 3″ square
- Burgundy: 3″ square
- Coral: 1″ × 3″ piece
- Green multitone background: fat eighth
- Pre-fused binding fabric: 3″ × 12″, cut into 3 strips ⅝″ × 12″
- Card stock: 9″ × 6″
- Thread colors: yellow; light, medium, and dark pinks; coral; light, medium, and dark greens; medium rosy-burgundy

CUTTING AND ASSEMBLY

For this project, I've already done the outlining, tracing, and pattern marking, so make 2 copies of the full-size master template on page 40. Use 1 for your master pattern and 1 to cut apart, or create your own from your original work (see page 38).

tip

> *Assess your pattern and decide whether there are some pieces you want to combine when you cut them. The details can be added back in later with thread. This would be an option for the burgundy center of the hibiscus.*

When cutting and placing your pattern pieces, make some rules for yourself about how you will proceed. For this hibiscus, I chose to cut each whole petal out of medium pink and then add the smaller pieces to the top of that fabric instead of cutting the small pieces and trying to assemble them without a base. The center stamen is also fused onto the completed flower, and the yellow fuzzy part is added with thread. You could also choose to do all the shading with thread and simply use a medium pink for the petals.

1. Cut out 1 petal at a time from the paper pattern, then select and cut the pre-fused fabric for that area. Use the dashed line as a cutting aid to indicate the edges that need extra fabric for underlap. Add ¼″ of fabric along these dashed line edges.

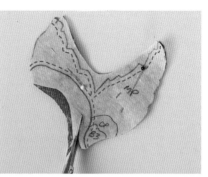

Pin and cut pattern pieces. Add ¼″ on edges where there is a dashed line.

2. Cut off the next largest piece of the petal on the paper pattern. In this case, cut on the line between the medium pink and the dark pink. Use that new pattern piece to cut out the dark pink fabric. Fuse in place.

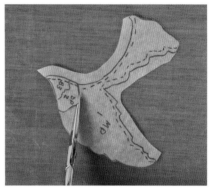

Cut apart pattern sections.

3. Repeat Step 2 for the burgundy part in the center of the flower.

4. Build each individual petal before adding the next petal. Use the master pattern as a guide to arrange and fuse the pieces.

Build flower petals.

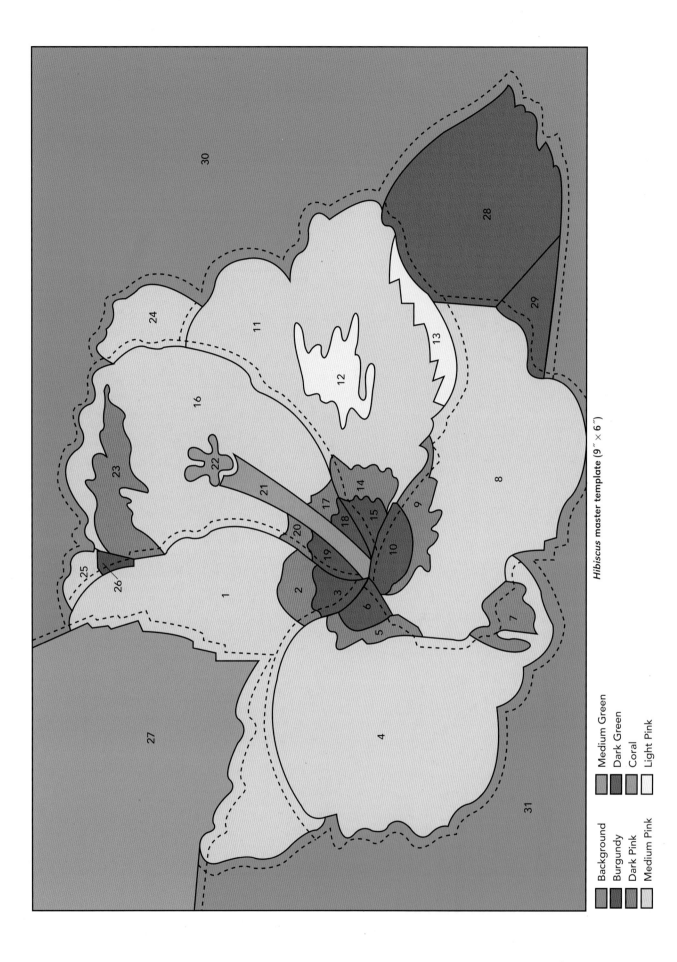

Hibiscus master template (9" × 6")

Background | Medium Green
Burgundy | Dark Green
Dark Pink | Coral
Medium Pink | Light Pink

tip

Before cutting out the pattern piece for the petal with the stamen in it, trace the stamen to use as your pattern. Then build the petal as if the stamen weren't there. Add it at the end.

5. Place the master pattern on your pressing surface. Cover it with a piece of parchment paper, and arrange the petal pieces on top. You should be able to see through the parchment paper well enough to use the master pattern as a placement guide.

6. As you place each petal piece in order, press it into place by tapping it quickly with a hot iron. After the pieces cool, they will lift off the parchment paper. Continue like this until the flower is complete.

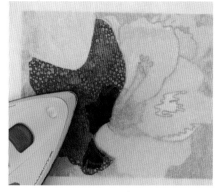

Place pattern pieces.

tip

The paper backing that comes with the fusible web product can be used in place of the parchment paper. Covering the newly cut pieces with release paper will keep your iron clean.

7. It is your choice whether or not to apply fusible web to the background pieces when using fast2fuse as your base. If the pieces are simple, you can just fuse them directly to the fast2fuse. If they have more intricate edges, you may want to apply the fusible web anyway because they will be easier to cut out. Apply the background pieces to the base, and fuse the flower subject on top; then fuse any remaining pieces, such as the top leaf.

Arrange background and flower pieces on fast2fuse.

tip

If your background is darker than your light-colored subject, press on just enough background so that the edges are covered by the subject. This will prevent bleed-through of the dark color to the subject.

8. With simple back-and-forth strokes of machine quilting, add accents to the flower, blending the colors with the thread. Stitch in the direction of the veins in the flower and leaves. Add the little yellow fuzzy part on the top of the stamen. Quilt the background area to look like more leaves if desired.

Thread painting and accents

9. See General Instructions, pages 13–15, for directions on finishing your Quilt-O-Gram.

GALLERY

Fall Harvest, 5″ × 7″,
by Lalece Rooker, 2007

This original design was inspired
by the bounty on display at a
roadside produce farm. Lalece
used lots of thread painting
and scrapbooking dots on
the sunflowers.

Butterfly Illusion, 9″ × 6″,
by Cheryl Malkowski, 2007

I loved the fussy-cut butterfly and wanted it to
stand out, so it is embellished with crystals and
bobbin work. The gerbera daisy in the background is traced from a photograph and
stitched with colored threads.

Believe, 4″ × 9″,
by Cheryl Malkowski, 2007

I wanted to feature metal
letters in a project. This
card uses batik and silver
lamé fabrics, holographic
thread, and bobbin work
with Superior's Razzle
Dazzle thread.

Orange Daisy, 8¾″ × 3¾″,
by Cheryl Malkowski, 2007

This is just for fun, playing with shapes and fussy-cut
motifs. I used lots of thread painting, including some
holographic thread and bobbin work.

Thank-You Bouquet, 6″ × 9″,
by Cheryl Malkowski, 2007

This bouquet is made from a collection of fussy-cut batik flowers. They are embellished with crystals, craft store ribbon, bobbin work, and a big "thank you" stamp.

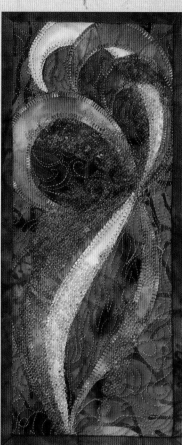

Fabric Dance, 4″ × 9″,
by Doris Koozer, 2007

This is simply a doodle on (and with) fabric, frosted with glass beads and stitched with decorative machine stitches.

Happy Thanksgiving, 5″ × 7″,
by Cheryl Malkowski, 2007

Inspired by the subtle leaf motif, I fussy cut, outlined with pretty thread, and stamped on my greeting.

Winter Welcome, 6″ × 9″,
by Shirley Pyle, 2007

Inspired by a snowman on an old greeting card, this Quilt-O-Gram features fussy-cut motifs and fancy machine stitches.

Snowy Greetings, 4³⁄₄″ × 6³⁄₄″,
by Barbara Watson, 2007

The scene from this piece of fabric reminded Barb of a Christmas card. It is lightly embellished with thread painting in the trees and snow.

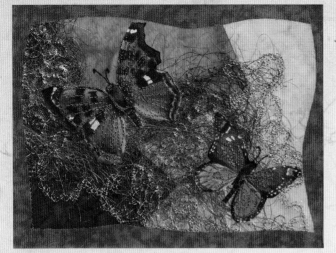

Togetherness, 6¾″ × 5⅛″,
by Barbara Watson, 2007

Fussy-cut butterflies inspired this Quilt-O-Gram featuring Angelina fibers, metallic thread, and a wavy binding.

Swimming with Friends, 8½″ × 6½″,
by Shirley Pyle, 2007

The big blue fish in the batik fabric inspired this project, and Shirley added free-cut plant life and little fish. Decorative stitching and bobbin work were used to embellish.

Shine, 6″ × 6″,
by Lalece Rooker, 2007

Lalece says she's always liked doodling sunshine motifs with original faces. She made this one using Pigma pens and crayons on fabric and embellishing with iron-on crystals.

Iris Serenity, 6″ × 9″, by Amy Vetter, 2007

Amy was inspired to make this Quilt-O-Gram by a photo of the iris gardens in Keizer, Oregon. She used personally hand-dyed fabrics and shimmering threads for accents and the spider web.

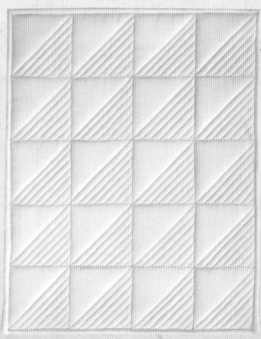

Shadows Play, 8″ × 10″,
by Ramonda "Charlie" Weckerle, 2007

Inspired by tile work, this piece was machine quilted with silk thread. An extra layer of cotton batting fused to the fast2fuse enhances the definition.

Luna Moth, 9″ × 6″, by Amy Vetter, 2007

Amy fondly remembers her dad's collection of butterflies and moths from when she was a child. She made this luna moth from batiks, embellished with satin stitching.

Follow Your Dreams, 5½″ × 3¾″, by Barbara Watson, 2007

Barbara was looking for a place to incorporate the craft ribbon's message and developed this design. This fussy-cut butterfly has a trail made by free-motion stitching on a zigzag setting.

Moorish Idol, 9″ × 6″, by Amy Vetter, 2007

Amy likes to play around with tropical fish fabric to make her own fantasy fish. This piece uses some fussy-cut sea life and rayon thread painting.

Snowflake Joy, 7″ × 6″, by Lalece Rooker, 2007

The cut-out snowflake is like the paper ones children cut. Lalece made it into a Christmas card using iron-on crystals and metallic thread.

Kittens in the Garden, 9″ × 7″, by Carol Evenson, 2007

Created from one piece of cute kitten fabric, Carol fussy cut and moved some elements so the kittens played together.

Thank Goodness for Friends, 8¼″ × 6¼″,
by Teri Wells, 2007

Fun fabrics are enhanced with stamps and decorative stitches to make a meaningful token of friendship.

Must Be Love, 7″ × 5″,
by Cheryl Seibel, 2007

This was the perfect opportunity to use the adorable pig fabric. It is embellished with stamped letters, heart buttons, and a binding cut with fancy-edged scissors.

BOO, 9¼″ × 7¼″, by Rosaley Smith, 2007

This Halloween Quilt-O-Gram was inspired by the fun fabric and is embellished with fussy-cut motifs, glitter, and a machine blanket stitch on the binding.

Pond Beauty, 6⅞″ × 6″,
by Barbara Watson, 2007

The water lily and leaf are fussy cut from beautiful fabric and fused to the batik. Barbara added crystals and thread painted using a zigzag stitch.

RESOURCES

For a list of other fine books from C&T Publishing, ask for a free catalog:

C&T Publishing, Inc.

P.O. Box 1456, Lafayette, CA 94549

(800) 284-1114

Email: ctinfo@ctpub.com

Website: www.ctpub.com

C&T Publishing's professional photography services are now available to the public. Visit us at www.ctmediaservices.com.

For quilting supplies:

Cotton Patch

1025 Brown Ave., Lafayette, CA 94549

(800) 835-4418 or

(925) 283-7883

Email: CottonPa@aol.com

Website: www.quiltusa.com

Note: Fabrics used in the quilts shown may not be currently available, as fabric manufacturers keep most fabrics in print for only a short time.

Most of the Quilt-O-Grams in this book were quilted with beautiful 40-weight premium high-sheen polyester and other specialty threads from Superior Threads. To check availability in your area, go to www.superiorthreads.com, and click on the store locator.

Superior Threads

P.O. Box 1672, St. George, UT 84771

(435) 652-1867

The Electric Quilt Company makes quilt design software and high-quality printable fabric sheets, which were used in making the Quilt-O-Gram no-sew mini-quilts in this book. Find the latest version of EQ software at your local quilt store or online at www.electricquilt.com.

The Electric Quilt Company

419 Gould Street, Suite 2, Bowling Green, OH 43402

(800) 356-4219

Most of the batik and hand-dyed fabrics featured throughout this book are from Timeless Treasures Fabrics. Ask for them at your local quilt shop, and visit www.ttfabrics.com to see the current offerings.

Timeless Treasures Fabrics, Inc.

483 Broadway, New York, NY 10013

(212) 226-1400

EK Success, Ltd., is a leader in the scrapbooking industry, providing fun designs for scrapbook makers as well as Quilt-O-Gram makers. Visit your local craft or scrapbooking store or the company's website, www.eksuccess.com, to see what's cool in the world of embellishments.

EK Success, Ltd.

www.eksuccess.com

Adobe Systems, Inc.

Adobe Photoshop Elements

www.adobe.com

Microsoft Corporation

Microsoft Word

Windows Media Player

www.microsoft.com

ABOUT THE AUTHOR

Photo courtesy of Terry Day

Cheryl Malkowski lives in Roseburg, Oregon, with her husband, Tom, and their dog, Bosco. She has two grown children and one grandchild, who is her favorite little boy.

This is her third book with C&T, and she likes writing almost as much as teaching.

She loves everything about the quilting process, especially the actual quilting, whether on a domestic machine or a longarm. Her quilting has been displayed at many shows, including the American Quilter's Society show in Paducah, Kentucky. Cheryl was a featured guest on The Quilt Show at www.thequiltshow.com in the inaugural season, which is available on DVD from that site.

Easy Chenille Appliqué and *Fun with One Block Quilts*, also by Cheryl, are available from C&T Publishing, Inc.

For information about Cheryl's pattern company, cheryl rose creations; workshops; lectures; and ways to contact her, visit www.cherylmalkowski.com.

DEDICATION

For every quilter who has an art quilter inside who's trying to get out.

APPRECIATION

What would I do without my wonderful quilting friends here in Roseburg, Oregon? The ladies of the Umpqua Valley Quilters Guild again made a significant contribution to the gallery in this book, as did the Tuesday Night Quilters' Frenzy group at Country Lady Quilt Shop. They are all truly inspirational.

The fine people at Timeless Treasures Fabrics supplied me with so many gorgeous batiks and hand-dyed fabrics that it was hard to choose which ones to use next. Thank you so much!

Superior Threads helped me figure out the best threads to use in different applications and then how to use them. The 40-weight polyester threads for decorative stitching and quilting on these Quilt-O-Grams are fabulous.

The Electric Quilt Company was gracious enough to send me some of its high-quality printable fabric sheets, which are perfect for making little Quilt-O-Grams of *That Quilt You Never Wanted to Make* (page 20). Used in conjunction with EQ6, the projects were practically done before I started them.

Thanks, EK Success, for the stamps and embellishments used in making these Quilt-O-Grams, and for opening my eyes to products available in the scrapbook industry that transfer so nicely to quilting. I *love* the Adornaments, which are little packages of fun, nubby yarns!

As always, the C&T staff is great to work with. I couldn't be happier to be associated with such wonderful, creative people. They also sent me some fast2fuse to work with. Who knew it was going to be so perfect for making Quilt-O-Grams?

My family is always very supportive of me and lets me have the time I need to get everything done. This book went by quickly, like the projects themselves, and Bosco, the dog, didn't even notice that he was being ignored, so he didn't have to go pout anywhere.

Great Titles

from 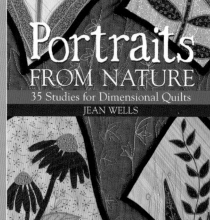 C&T PUBLISHING

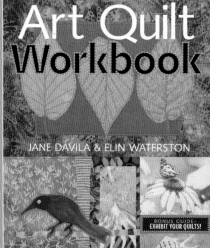
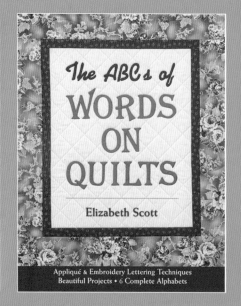